Dear Fellow Early Reader:

This book promotes the "I can" attitude and promotes early reading and learning.

We offer to you the mantra that we recite with confidence when "I can do much, much with great skill. I can do much when I have the will.

Where there is a will, there is a way. I have the will in me today!"

Rajah-Nia is so well-mannered,
and often wants to help.
She is independent and only wants assistance
after she has been allowed to try it herself.

By climbing on her laundry stool to change the washer loads,

Rajah has learned to wash, dry, and fold, **properly** caring for her clothes.

Rajah has learned to help big brother wash dishes with no **hesitation**.

In the sink she places cups before plates, learning about **preparation**.

"I can do it!"

Rajah's can-do **attitude** helps her **confidence** improve.

"I can do it, Mommy. With a little trust, let me try it, Mommy. I am big enough.

I am not a baby. I am all of 4 and though I may be little, I can do a little more."

Rajah is very special and super-smart, indeed.

Because Rajah-Nia, at four years old, has already learned to read!

THINK AND GROW RICH

Not only can Rajah read sight words like dog, log, and tent.

She can, too, read big words like **creativity** and **acknowledgment**.

Dog

Log

Tent

Acknowledgement

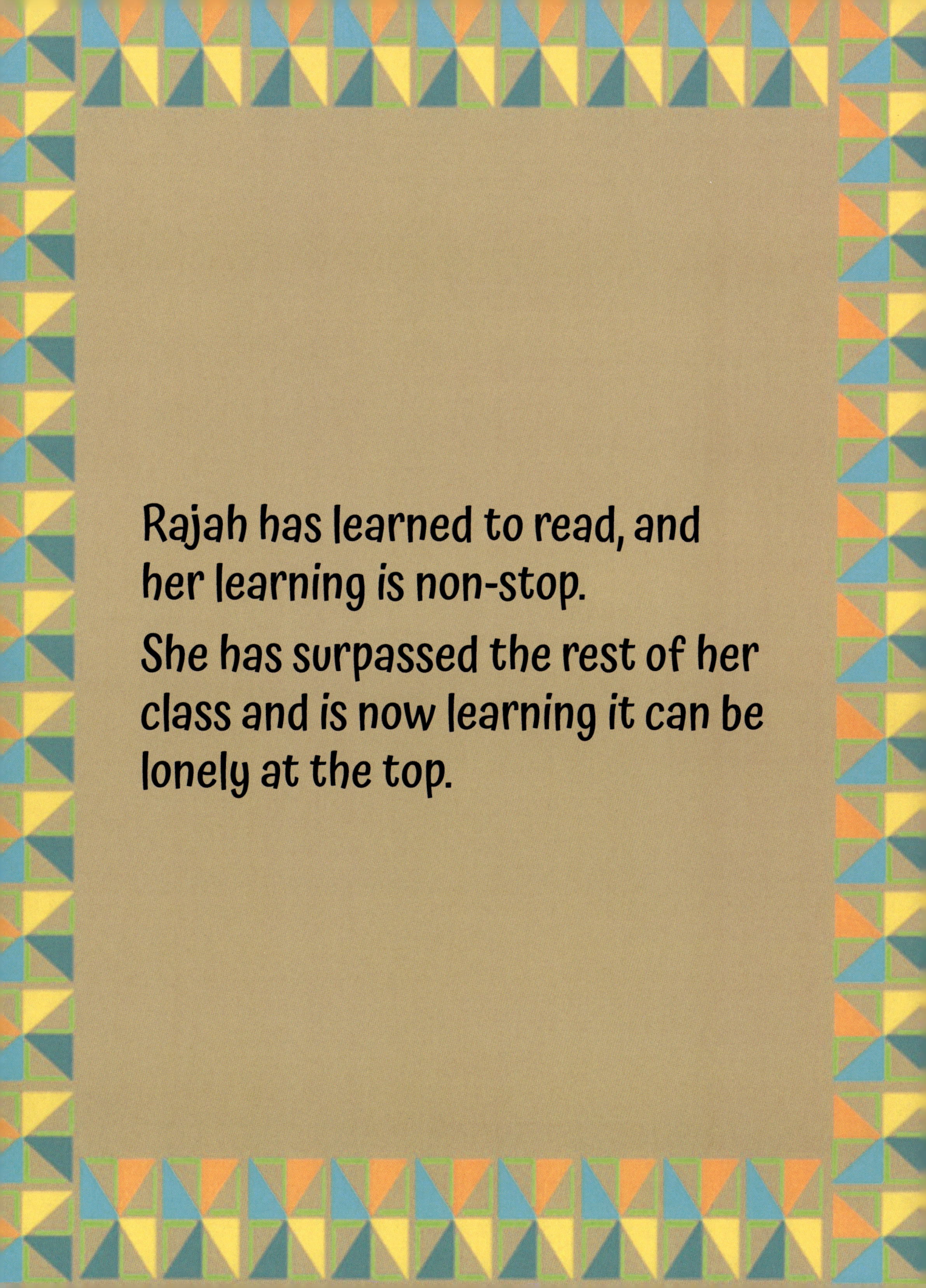

Rajah has learned to read, and her learning is non-stop.

She has surpassed the rest of her class and is now learning it can be lonely at the top.

She finishes her work early even though she is 2 grades ahead, and she is the only one who has nap time while the others have recess instead.

Being smart is hard even though the work is easy, especially at 4 when you know much more than need be.

Rajah can keep up with the lessons, but the older children are so much more mature, it can be hard to **navigate** friendship when one is 7 and the other is 4.

Today Rajah feels nervous and just a tad bit sad. Because Mommy is moving her from Madam Oppong's Montessori class.

"Cheer up, Rajah," says Mommy. "All of your friends' phone numbers are the same.

However, you cannot grow from learning what you already know, so your routine will have to change.

Mommy will be your teacher again, just like we used to do, and a few times each week, we will meet with others whose mommies are their teachers, too.

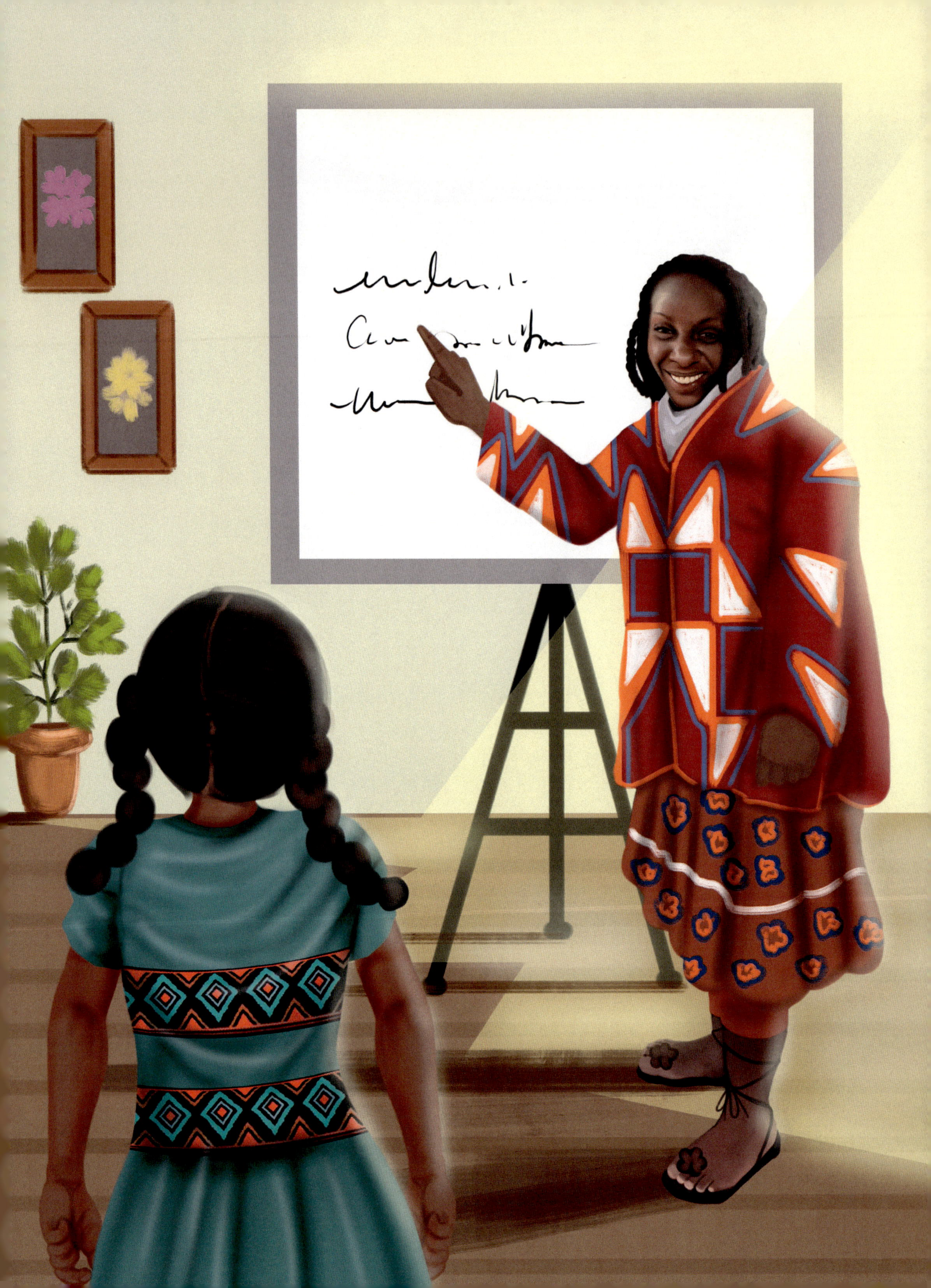

You will be learning new things while still getting the challenge that you need;

Making many new friends your age but most importantly your learning speed."

Rajah knows that learning is when she 'understands something new' and speed means 'how fast.'

So she decided she might try to hide it, and then maybe she could remain in Madam Oppong's class.

"What if I slowed down learning? Then could I stay in school?"

"That's not an option," said Mommy.
"Remember our golden rule?"

"Yes! I am star-essence and a chosen one for greater,
I smile bright, and I aim high because I am a **CREATOR**!"

"Very good!" said Mommy. "You must always remember, too.

You were created for Mommy, and Mommy is made for you.

I know this is a big step, and changing **routines** is hard.

But you are more ready for this than you think you are."

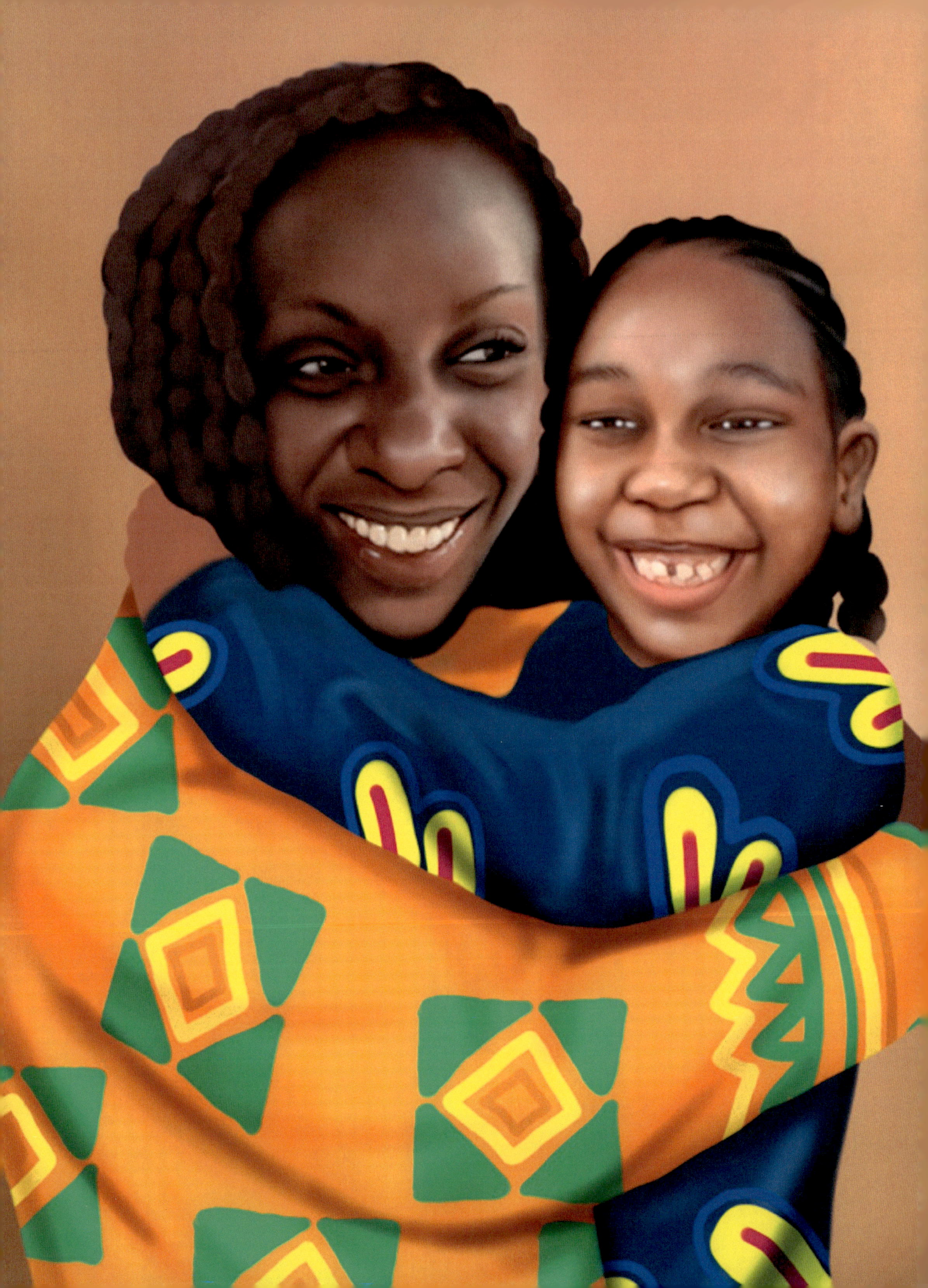

Can you trust Mommy on this, or is this job a little too tough?

"Yes!" said Rajah, "I can do it, Mommy. I am big enough!

I am not a baby. I am all of 4. And although I may be little, I can do a little more."

And Rajah did do better home schooled, by much more than a little bit. She is known as Rajah-Nia The Early Reader, and she is very proud of it!

I can do anything

Let's Review!

1. What is so special about Rajah?

2. What happens to Rajah while the other children are at recess?

3. What is Rajah's favorite thing to tell her mommy?

4. Wich task does Rajah do with assistance?

5. What is Rajah have to move from Madam Oppong's Class?

6. Why does Rajah have to move from Madam Oppong's Class?

7. What are some things that you like to do that can be helpful to others?

8. Why do you think Rajah-Nia is so capable?

9. What has this book taught you?

10. If you could write a book about yourself, what would you write about?

GLOSSARY WORDS and DEFINITIONS

1. Creativity: (noun) — the ability to make or invent something original or imaginative.

2. Acknowledgment (noun) — the act of showing appreciation or thanks for something.

3. Properly: (noun) — correctly.

4. Navigate: (verb) — to plan, manage, or control the course of.

5. Hesitation: (verb) — to move slowly because of not being sure.

6. Preparation: (noun) — the act or process of getting ready.

7. Routines: (noun) — an activity or activities done regularly.

8. Attitude: (noun) — a feeling or mental state.

9. Confidence: (noun) — having trust or confidence.

10. Creator: (noun) one who creates.

Source: Free On-Line English Dictionary | Thesaurus |

Children's, Intermediate

Dictionary | Wordsmyth

MEET THE AUTHORS

RAJAH-NIA & MOM

THANK YOU!

"Medase" to my Mom, and Dad for instilling the love of reading, words, and learning as fun.

You, Ms. Dollyah, for making my book for me. (R-NT)

SCAN ME

Made in the USA
Middletown, DE
27 December 2024